Animals Do, Too!

How They Behave Just Like You

Written by **Etta Kaner**

Illustrated by **Marilyn Faucher**

Kids Can Press

Do you like to **dance**?

Honeybees do, too!

Honeybees dance to tell other bees where to find a tasty meal, like a flower with lots of sweet nectar. If the flower is close by, the bee dances in a circle. If it's farther away, the bee does a waggle dance in the shape of an 8. The bee can also show the direction of the nectar by angling its body toward or away from the sun.

Do you like to **play tag**?

Gazelles do, too!

Gazelles like to take turns chasing and being chased. But for these swift animals, tag is not just a game — it's also useful. When young gazelles play tag, they build up their strength and speed. This is important when escaping from predators (animals that eat them) on the open plains.

Do you like to **play leapfrog**?

Cattle egrets do, too!

More than just fun, leapfrog is how cattle egrets forage for food. The flock divides into two groups. The back group jumps over the front group to catch insects. This stirs up many more insects from the tall grasses. These insects fly up and are caught by the group following close behind. In this way, cattle egrets all get their fair share of food.

Do you like to **blow bubbles**?

Gray tree frogs do, too!

These tiny frogs make bubble nests in trees above water. The females produce a sticky liquid. Then, they kick at the liquid with their strong hind legs. The kicking pushes air into the liquid, just like when you blow bubbles in the bath. This creates a bubble nest where the female can lay her eggs. A few days later, the tadpoles hatch. They drop into water below the nest where they will grow into frogs.

Do you like to **grow food** in the garden?

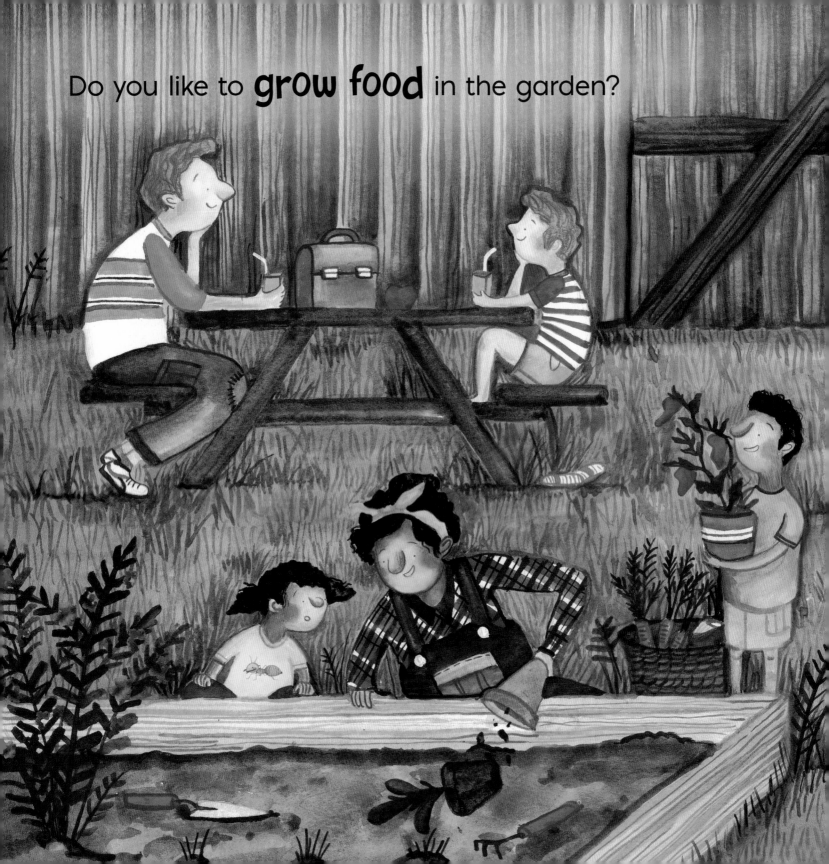

Leaf-cutter ants do, too!

These tropical insects work together to grow food for their ant colony. First, they carry freshly cut leaf pieces to their underground nest. Then, they lick the leaves and cut them up into smaller pieces. The ants chew these pieces into a mush that they plant in their nest. The mush helps grow a white fungus (like mushrooms) that the ants eat.

Do you like **piggyback rides**?

Marmosets do, too!

Baby marmosets get around by riding piggyback. Usually, two babies are born at the same time. Together, the newborns weigh half as much as their mother. That's a big load for her to carry, especially when she's out looking for food. So the father and older siblings help out. They carry the babies on their backs while the mother is out hunting.

Do you have a **babysitter**?

Flamingos do, too!

While flamingo parents hunt for food, they leave their chicks in the care of other flamingos. There can be thousands of baby flamingos in one crèche, or nursery. That's a lot of birds to keep an eye on! When the parents return, they have no problem finding their offspring — they just listen for their chick's call. Each one is different.

More About the Animals in This Book

Honeybees are a type of insect found around the world. They make and store honey for the winter, when there is no nectar to eat from fresh flowers.

Gazelles are a kind of antelope from Africa and Asia. These quick runners can reach 60 miles (97 kilometers) an hour — more than twice the speed of the fastest human!

Cattle egrets are a type of small heron that live in the world's fields and wetlands. They like to hunt near cattle (cows), whose hooves stir up prey in the grass below.

Gray tree frogs that make bubble nests live in Africa. They can appear gray, brown or white, and can camouflage themselves to blend in with their surroundings.

Leaf-cutter ants live mostly in the warm climates of Central and South America. Small but mighty, these heavy lifters can carry leaves that are fifty times their body weight!

Marmosets are a kind of monkey from Central and South America. The pygmy marmoset is the smallest monkey in the world. It can fit in an adult human's hand!

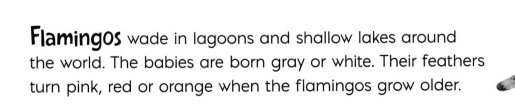

Flamingos wade in lagoons and shallow lakes around the world. The babies are born gray or white. Their feathers turn pink, red or orange when the flamingos grow older.

For Benjamin — you light up our lives! — E.K.
To my mother, who shared with me her love of animals — M.F.

Acknowledgments

Publishing a book is always a team effort and even more so in this case. A heartfelt thank you to Katie Scott for her attention to detail, creativity and good humor, to Marilyn Faucher for her endearing illustrations and to Michael Reis and Marie Bartholomew for their design.

Kids Can Press gratefully acknowledges the financial support of the Government of Ontario, through the Ontario Media Development Corporation; the Ontario Arts Council; the Canada Council for the Arts; and the Government of Canada, through the CBF, for our publishing activity.

Published in Canada and the U.S. by Kids Can Press Ltd.
25 Dockside Drive, Toronto, ON M5A 0B5

Kids Can Press is a Corus Entertainment Inc. company

www.kidscanpress.com

The artwork in this book was rendered in watercolor.
The text is set in Pontiac and Squidtoonz.

Edited by Katie Scott
Designed by Michael Reis

Printed and bound in Malaysia in 10/2016 by Tien Wah Press (Pte.) Ltd.

CM 17 0 9 8 7 6 5 4 3 2 1

Library and Archives Canada Cataloguing in Publication

Kaner, Etta, author
Animals do, too! : how they behave just like you / written by Etta Kaner ; illustrated by Marilyn Faucher.

ISBN 978-1-77138-569-5 (hardback)

1. Animal behavior — Juvenile literature. I. Faucher, Marilyn, 1989–, illustrator II. Title.

QL751.5.K363 2017   j591.5   C2016-902689-2